SONflowers for Faye

Torey Isaac

BookLeaf Publishing

Presentation by *BookLeaf Publishing*

Web: www.bookleafpub.com

E-mail: info@bookleafpub.com

ISBN: 9789357740524

First edition 2023

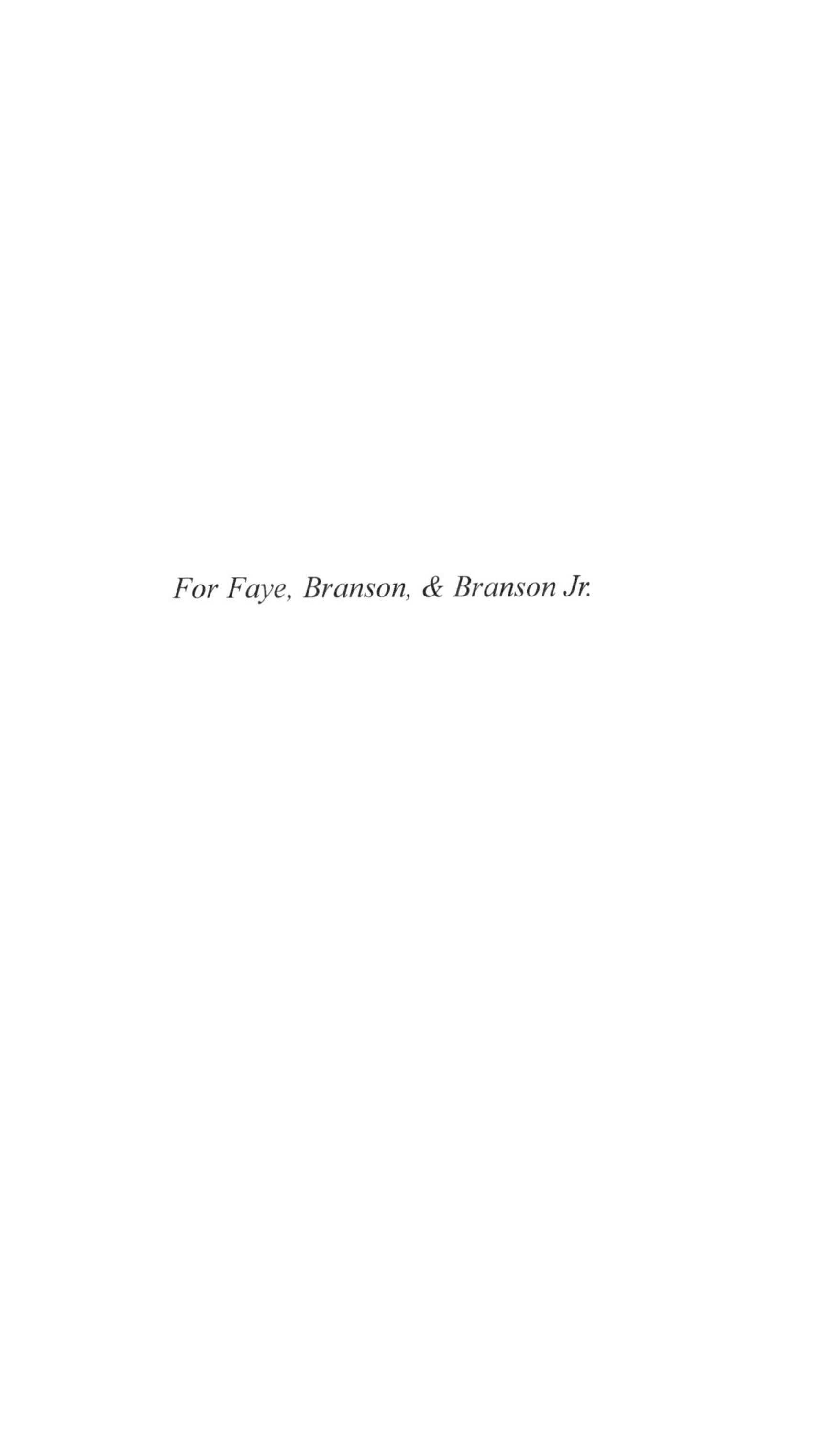

For Faye, Branson, & Branson Jr.

ACKNOWLEDGEMENT

To the courageous authors before myself, the thriving authors of now, & the future innovators of literary art form!

PREFACE

I had to give myself a pivotal push to introduce a dynamic and impactful body of work to the world. I wanted to tell my mother's story briefly and in a poetic way. This moment marks the fruition of my first book and a way to give my mother her flowers. This collection of poems is personal, celebratory, and intricately fit together to present a bouquet of gratitude & appreciation.

CONTENTS

i.l.y.f.m.

Garden

To grow into a flower
From a seed
That was not supposed to sprout after mother
nature had done away with her
Or at least she thought
Not thinking
That she would grow into a flower
Through the rain
And through all of life's rainstorms
She never looked for the rainbow that she
deserved
She never knew
Or had heard
What a beautiful flower she was blossoming into
Her floral life fragrance had only
Been smelled and admired
And later in life, she would learn
That she was appreciated
And she used those vital components
To grow two flowers
In an unorthodox garden

20:23

As one year left
Another presented itself
Young, fresh, and new
Vibrant and full of life
And innocent in its youth

I listened
On the other end of the phone
Initially 7 minutes
Turned into a conversation
Listening to you
Holding on to you
Trying to grasp
Everything
Recording my mind's memories
To cherish
To have
To hold

Even those private moments
That were yours
But now mines

From state to state
And traveled roads

While waiting for you to chime in

But you didn't
And you may never know

That I spent a little more time
With you
As you prayed
And thanked God

For another chance
Another glance
Another year

Glow/Golden Fields II

Glow:

It's the only way I can cope
God bless my mechanism
To craft
To create hope
Through forms of journalism

Years from now we'll talk about your glow
Your presence
Your effervescence

The way you left
Unknown
You are a lifelong blessing

I'll take these lessons now
Applying as I go
What you taught I'll make my own
Perfecting my own glow

...

Golden Fields II:

Running free
In those same golden fields
Only this time
The hue is yellow energy fantastic.
We are magnetic
As we have always been.
Your warmth, bright
And burning stupendously as a star.
These are the memories
The dreams
Sweet daydreams that are to come.

This will be how I remember

Steel Magnolia

Although I manifested life
The inevitable was on the horizon
She had been caged
And lived a caged life

A Steel Magnolia
Trapped behind a steel frame
She carried burden
She sadly harbored shame

She mailed joy
By way of m&m water colored cards
She wrote letters
Poetic in her own way

She had flown
But never to a limitless infinity
A hardened life
Tried to tell her of her identity

She was on the edge
A bittersweet conundrum
To let her go, to let her fly
So that she could live true freedom

These Days

These days
The conversations are longer
The faith is made stronger
The lessons are learned separately,
simultaneously.
I listen more
You talk more, we laugh
And you open up more
I hold on
You hold on, we reminisce
And we learn to cherish
And crave and bask in the right now
Because you never know these days.
The days are long
The long ones seem short when we're happy
And rather slow when sad
Drifting and dragging along
Distance makes us feel alone
But a simple call or text or chat
Makes it better
These days

Gentleness

For gentleness,
Reminders would come along
To provide inspiration.
Little glimpses of yellow
Would constantly dance across
My life timeline

Shining its vibrancy and warmth

Yellow's energy was constantly trending
Whispering to me
Write it out loud
Spill your emotions
Pour your heart into the pages
Of your mother's memoir.
Write about her
even if she is mad at you
Write about her goodness
Write about the flowers
And build up the garden
You will place at her feet,
Write about the flowers you'll give to her in
bouquets
In abundance
Saying thank you momma!

For all of the love
All of the good times
All of the lessons
And I'll even give you flowers
For the times you didn't think
You were worthy of a floral offering
In trenches
In darkness
Even in the concrete stone soil
Flowers can grow
Exuding beauty in uncanny places

Sunflower Heart

On that day
We'll wear sunflowers
And our eyes will shower the petals
And the dust will be scattered
And that will be goodbye

I'll dress you in yellow sunbeam
Your frequency will gleam

For in my heart
The deepest soil vessel
Is blessed with a seed
My blood will now flow yellow
My atriums sealed with petals
And my smile will also be filled with light
And your warmth
That you gave
And passed on to me
To my brother
To his son
And those who have sailed on

Upon my skin will be a tattoo
Of the very plant
That my mother nature gave to me

Beautiful Strife

Through positive speak
Impossible feats
are possible.
I was born to write your story
From your words
Through your eyes
To my pen
I placed it on paper
What you kept in.
How you felt
And sometimes spoke, but would hate to say.
From the darkest to the lightest
That made and makes you Faye.
I listened
As you candidly told me stories of
The past that helped mold you
I went thru all the feels as my mother
Told me her life's glory
Story by story
The ever so open
Open book
Helped craft your story
And fill your pages
From chapter
After chapter

I watched the way you lit up
As you told your own story

I was the News Reporter
Interviewing a rare story
That not everyone had exclusive access to.
I was front row and center
Over wine and birthday dinners
And got to meet different versions of you.

So on this day Momma
You can add author to your life
This is how you make beautiful art
Even out of strife

Pray

She taught us to pray.
Little did she know
Faye taught us faith.
Just to have a little bit
And with that little bit, you could go a long way.

"Say this prayer wherever you are,
Each and every night"

It built a bond
It created a chain
It was life continuity
Mapping out a journey of far roads

To interweave
Like deeper strands
To entangle our brotherly bond

And to know that
Whenever bedtime was near
My brother and I
Together or apart
Prayed the same prayer
Taught to us by our mother
For our hearts to never part

SONflowers

For even in the nights
That she couldn't
And when they were far away
God had set in place
Important things and people we needed along
the way

We grew from day to day
Sometimes moving from place to place
We felt it all.
Emotions that caused a change to the face
Feelings that nothing or no things could erase

There were struggles
There were tears
There were back and forth tug- o-wars
And phone conversations between adults over
where the boys would stay
and when the boys could play
And which parts of the dirty bad
That one could, and could not say.

To shield them
To protect them
To lessen the sadness

To quiet the madness
So that we did not have to grow up too soon
So that we could be better, stronger brothers
To build our love for each other

There were sacrifices made
And plenty of conversations
And even arguments
All of which were required to
Grow and shower
Faye's sonflowers

Momma Affirmations

This piece was originally entitled " A letter to young Faye"
It was jotted down
As words and thoughts
Then written in 2 days
These are my words
My take on the words you may not be able to find or say.
Before she met me
My old soul
My heart
My love
Whispered to her to say:

1. Momma! It's ok, hang on and continue to be strong!
2. You are wonderfully made.
3. Your life will be filled with SONflowers and Sunflowers
4. You are BE. YOU. TIFUL
5. Branson loves you!
6. You are deserving of everything good that God has for you!
7. Torey loves you!
8. You are a Queen

9. Your love and the way you love is contagious
10. Your presence is a present and needed for the
future!
11. Your story is important because it is my
story too and my legacy!

May my confirmations
Forever be your affirmations!

Petals

I gathered all of
The scattered petals
And made an offering
To show appreciation
And I exclaimed
"Here Momma
Happy Birthday!"
These flowers are for you
She smiled
She laughed
She cried
She felt love
--deeply
From a bouquet
Made abstractly
Of individual petals
With Love

A street named Faye

Deep in the heart of South Dallas, Texas
Exist a street
Rough and rugged
Rigid and rare
Lays a street
That reminds me of your name
I've never gone down this road
But if it's anything like the path we have traveled
It is nothing less of extraordinary

I look at this street sometimes.
Passing by and saying
"There's my mother's street!"
Her own piece of Texas
Her home is peace in Texas
It's resilient
And concrete wild
And tells the story of
And reflects the boldness of
And shows the beauty of
My yellow rose that grew
In Texas

Apple

I am the apple
Of your eye
That did not fall too far from the tree.
Our cores are the same
We are linked
Our love is not forbidden fruit
But yet a plentiful harvest
Of crops reaped
From sown seeds.
I am an apple
Refreshing
And delightful in season
And patiently pending
Slow-grown perfection in the off-season.
I am the apple
That did not fall too far
Not even in distance
Not even in spirit
Not even in love
I am the apple
Connected to my mother

Family Ties

Unbound by family ties
You found other ways to water your sons

Along the way, we learned to let friends become
our family leaves

You only met your mother through pictures,
your sister through a visit and had spoken with
your brother on the phone

Our family seeds were scattered

I knew not of my history
Although I was born of legacy
My lineage was royalty
And rich in spirit

My Great Grandmother's silk skin
was passed down to every beautiful hued brown
beauty gem in my family

Our Topaz skin tells a story of self-love
Self-Care
And the reality of those two things
Mixed with struggle and strife

Our lovely bones were made to withstand blow
after mighty blow

My DNA together with
My family's blood, sweat, tears
Heartache and trauma
Gifted curses
Signed in diamond life cursive

Draped like hand me downs
To pass on
And on and on

To legacies known and
Those unborn

And that they may continue to share stories of
the ones before them
The royal ones
From whom their brown fruit, or brown crop
was picked

May we all continue to be
To be legacy

To be timeless pictures in the frame
Or spirit felt whispers to speak our family name

Hallmark Tears

Hallmark Cards make her cry
Words read silently speak volumes out loud
Speaking loud
and of how
Monumental her presence has been in respective
lives.

She feels proud!

Her tear ducts fill up.
Water pours from the wells of her eyes
On her mantle
On a counter
Are a collection of those who love her
Cards kept as trinkets
From years gone and past
These cards are loved ones
Afterthoughts
Gentle reminders
And random acts of kindness
And love

The Water

I go to the water for her
In places she may never see
Be it ocean, lake, river, sea
It reminds me of the many tears she's cried
Be it sad, joyful, mad, or laughter

The water is her, my mother
close to me
Even when many miles away

I stare in amazement
I take it in
In silence
While my mind writes the next
Lines of my next great work

Her tears have inspired a son
Her tears have written poems
Her tears have moved generation after
generation
Her tears have shown human vulnerability
And the capability of letting go
Her tears have fought droughts
Pouring, running, and streaming oceans, lakes,
rivers, and even the 7 seas

I find her in the water
My mother. The water. Me.

August 5th

My world stopped only to start again.
A new sunflower sprung up from
The ground and from the soil of his mother's
belly and his father's seeds
He is the firstborn third

She had cursed him and pushed him away
because she was torn
Like her fingers that were constantly pricked by
thorns
Amends would place the garden back on strong
soil
To create and continue royal cultivation
His uncle had a hard day but the joy of his
arrival made the test of the day irrelevant
He was perfect
The way his father smiled at him for the first
time
There was a gleam in his eyes
A beam of light for a little bright light
My brother, now a young man
Eternally remains a youth
A photo of a kid brother
In my mind
Even though he is four years my junior

And now he holds his namesake

I crowned him with the words
"I am proud of you"
And prayed and spoke
Of well speak for my nephew and his mother

May God forever bless his little born majesty

Throne

Summer returned
Reincarnated new lifeform
Now new life
New hope
New beginnings
Things all projecting newness

Sooner than an expected September
He pushed his way through
Ready to meet his lineage of greatness
Ready to claim his heir
Ready to claim his crown as a young prince
A new lifeline
A new brilliant heartbeat
A new joy
Who shall become a King one day

LOVE.

I show
I express
I feel
I reside
In love
Because it is all and everything that you have
instilled in me.
It's everything that I am
And the parts of you
That shines through me.
It starts & ends with love
You have provided it unconditionally,
Definitively,
Infinite
In Abundance
Submerged and smothered
By your love.
You have rendered this unto me
At no cost
But had it a price
You'd pay in love if you could.
So as I go through my day
I pay it forward and pass on my
Little pieces of Faye
To strangers

To friends
And family too.
It is not always perfect
But kind and forgiving
with a tiny bit of patience.
If I ever lack it for myself
Or if I ever need it
I know that I can get it from you
Through a card
A call
A hug
An embrace
Or a simple soft-spoken salutation.
Signed
Sealed
And delivered in
LOVE.

Have you ever admired a Sunflower?

Have you ever admired a Sunflower?
Its beauty far and fair
She's like the outcast flower
Radiantly rare.
She beams
She reflects the sun
She's vibrant if you dare.
Letting light shine through
Your life window
Without a single care.
Next time you see a Sunflower
Stop and take a beat.
Breathe in,
Thank God and smile
A flower,
Simply neat!